MONEY MARKET INVESTING 101

A BEGINNER'S GUIDE TO LOW-RISK SHORT-TERM INVESTMENTS

Usiere Uko

...To new frontiers, learning and growing

CONTENTS

INTRODUCTION

A BEGINNER'S GUIDE TO LOW-RISK SHORT-TERM INVESTMENTS

Welcome to Money Market Investing 101: A Beginner's Guide to Low-Risk Short-Term Investments. In this book, we embark on a journey into the world of money market investing, where safety, liquidity, and modest returns converge to provide a secure foundation for your financial growth.

As a beginner in the realm of investing, you may find the landscape overwhelming and complex, with a myriad of options vying for your attention. The money market offers a compelling starting point for those seeking a low-risk introduction to the world of finance. Its focus on short-term, highly liquid instruments provides a safe haven for preserving capital while offering the potential to earn attractive, albeit moderate, returns.

In this comprehensive guide, we will demystify the intricacies of money market investing, breaking down complex concepts into easily digestible morsels of knowledge. Whether you are a young professional setting aside your first dollars for investment or a seasoned saver looking to optimize your portfolio, this book is designed to provide you with the essential tools to make informed and confident decisions.

Throughout these pages, we will explore the various types of money market instruments available, from Treasury Bills and

Certificates of Deposit to Money Market Funds and Repurchase Agreements. Each investment option will be dissected, revealing its unique features, benefits, and potential risks, empowering you to choose the ones that best align with your financial goals.

As we delve into the mechanics of money market investments, we will also discuss how to assess risk effectively. Understanding the relationship between risk and return is paramount in constructing a robust money market portfolio that suits your risk tolerance and objectives.

Beyond the fundamentals, we will guide you in developing a sound investment strategy, helping you define your financial goals and create a diversified money market portfolio that aligns with your aspirations. Moreover, we will address crucial topics such as tax considerations, the role of financial advisors, and the best practices for managing your investments effectively.

Investing is a journey, and as with any journey, there will be obstacles and uncertainties along the way. However, armed with knowledge, prudence, and an eagerness to learn, you will gain the confidence to navigate the money market landscape and thrive as an investor.

As you turn the pages of this book, you will not only discover the art of money market investing but also develop a deep understanding of how it fits into your financial portfolio. While the money market offers stability and security, we will also explore the opportunities for growth that extend beyond its boundaries.

Let us embark on this journey together and embark on the path towards financial empowerment through *Money Market Investing 101: A Beginner's Guide to Low-Risk Short-Term Investments.*

PART 1: INTRODUCTION TO MONEY MARKET INVESTING

1: UNDERSTANDING THE MONEY MARKET

Welcome to the exciting world of money market investing. In this chapter, we'll embark on a journey to understand the fundamental concepts that form the bedrock of the money market and why it holds such importance in the world of finance.

At its core, the money market is a specialized segment of the financial market where short-term debt instruments are bought and sold. These instruments have maturities of *one year or less*, making them highly liquid and providing investors with the flexibility to access their funds quickly.

The primary objective of the money market is to facilitate the smooth flow of money and maintain stability in the financial system. Various participants, such as governments, corporations, and financial institutions, actively engage in money market transactions to meet their short-term funding requirements and manage cash surpluses.

Let's explore some key characteristics of the money market:

Short-Term Nature: As mentioned earlier, money market instruments have short maturities, ranging from a few days to up to a year. This short-term nature offers a level of safety and predictability, as investors do not have to lock their money away for extended periods.

Low Risk: Money market instruments are considered relatively safe due to their short maturities and high credit quality. Government-backed securities, for example, are typically seen as low-risk investments.

High Liquidity: Liquidity refers to the ease of converting an asset into cash without significantly affecting its price. Money market instruments are highly liquid, ensuring that investors can access their funds quickly when needed.

Modest Returns: While the safety and liquidity of money market investments are appealing, they usually offer modest returns compared to riskier asset classes like stocks or long-term bonds. However, these returns are still higher than what traditional savings accounts typically offer.

Diverse Range of Instruments: The money market encompasses a diverse array of instruments, each serving unique purposes. Treasury Bills, Certificates of Deposit, and Commercial Paper are just a few examples of these instruments.

For many individuals, knowing where to invest their hard-earned savings can be a daunting challenge. Thankfully, the money market presents an excellent starting point for their investment journey. With its inherently low-risk nature compared to other investment options, the money market offers a secure and stable environment to begin building their financial portfolio.

Understanding the money market is a crucial first step in your investment journey. It provides a solid foundation for building your financial knowledge and making informed decisions. As we progress through this book, you'll explore each money market instrument in detail, gaining valuable insights into their characteristics, benefits, and risks.

Whether you're a novice investor looking to preserve your capital or a seasoned saver seeking short-term investment opportunities, the money market has something to offer.

2: BENEFITS OF MONEY MARKET INVESTMENTS

Within your financial security portfolio, the money market holds a crucial role. In this chapter, we will explore the myriad advantages that money market investments bring to the table. By understanding these benefits, you will gain insight into why the money market is a favored choice among investors who prioritize stability and safety while still seeking reasonable returns.

PRESERVATION OF CAPITAL

One of the primary benefits of money market investments lies in their exceptional ability to preserve capital. As investors, safeguarding our hard-earned money is of utmost importance, and money market instruments excel in offering precisely that.

When you allocate your funds to money market instruments, such as Treasury Bills, Certificates of Deposit (CDs), or Money Market Funds, you can rest assured that your principal investment amount is secure. These short-term instruments are designed to minimize the risk of capital loss, making them a favored choice for those seeking stability and protection of their wealth.

While it's crucial to acknowledge that no investment is entirely risk-free, money market investments are renowned for their low-risk profile compared to more volatile assets like stocks or long-term bonds. The short maturities of these instruments, typically ranging from a few days to one year, ensure that your money is not tied up for extended periods, minimizing exposure to market fluctuations.

The low-risk nature of money market investments is primarily attributed to the issuers' high credit quality and the instruments' short durations. Treasury Bills, for instance, are backed by the credit of the government, making them virtually risk-free. Even in cases where money market instruments are issued by corporations or municipalities, credit risk is often minimal due to thorough credit evaluations and high credit ratings.

This preservation of capital aspect in money market investing is especially appealing to risk-averse investors, retirees, or those saving for short-term financial goals. By choosing money market investments, you strike a balance between the desire for reasonable returns and the need for security, providing peace of mind as you navigate the financial landscape.

PREDICTABLE RETURNS

A key advantage of money market investments is the predictability they offer in generating returns. For investors who prioritize stability and a steady income stream, money market instruments prove to be a reliable choice.

Unlike the often unpredictable and volatile nature of the stock market, money market investments follow a more straightforward and dependable trajectory. These short-term instruments are designed to provide consistent returns over their relatively brief maturity periods, typically ranging from a few days to one year. This predictability is particularly valuable for individuals who seek to preserve capital while also earning a reasonable income on their investments.

The consistency of returns in money market investments can be attributed to several factors. Firstly, these instruments are characterized by their high credit quality as stated earlier.

Secondly, money market instruments are short-term in nature, which minimizes exposure to interest rate fluctuations and market volatility. As these instruments mature relatively quickly, any potential changes in interest rates have a limited impact on the returns they offer. Investors can rest assured that their earnings are relatively stable and not subject to the wide swings experienced in longer-term investments.

This predictability of returns provides peace of mind to investors, especially those with short-term financial goals or who rely on a stable income stream. Retirees, for instance, often opt for money market investments to supplement their retirement income while safeguarding their capital from significant market risks.

While money market investments offer consistent returns, these returns may be relatively modest compared to more aggressive investment options like stocks. As with any investment strategy, balancing risk and reward is vital, and money market investments fulfill the role of a stable anchor in a well-diversified portfolio.

DIVERSE INVESTMENT OPTIONS

One of the compelling features of the money market is its ability to provide a diverse array of investment instruments, catering to a wide spectrum of risk appetites and preferences. As an investor exploring the money market, you are presented with a rich selection of options from Treasury Bills backed by governments to Commercial Paper issued by corporations, each tailored to suit your unique financial goals and objectives.

The wide range of money market instruments available allows you to tailor your investment strategy to match your risk tolerance, financial objectives, and time horizon. Whether you seek the safety of government-backed securities or the potential for slightly higher returns from corporate debt, the money market accommodates various preferences.

FLEXIBILITY IN INVESTMENT AMOUNTS

One of the appealing features of money market investments is the flexibility they offer in terms of investment amounts. Unlike some traditional investment options that may have high minimum requirements, the money market presents a more accessible and inclusive landscape, accommodating investors with varying budget sizes.

Low Minimum Investment Requirements: Money market instruments, such as Treasury Bills, Certificates of Deposit (CDs), and Money Market Funds, often come with low minimum investment thresholds. This means that individuals can participate in the money market with relatively modest initial investments, making it feasible for a wide range of investors, including those with limited funds to enter the market.

Opportunity for Small Investors: The low minimum investment requirements in the money market create opportunities for small investors to get started on their investment journey. Whether you're just beginning to save or have a modest disposable income, money market investments provide a way to set aside a portion of your savings and put it to work without the need for substantial capital.

Gradual Portfolio Building: For those seeking to build their investment portfolio gradually, money market investments offer a convenient and incremental approach. Investors can allocate funds to money market instruments on a regular basis, slowly accumulating a diverse range of short-term assets over time.

Inclusive Participation: The flexibility in investment amounts makes the money market an inclusive and welcoming space for a broad spectrum of individuals. It accommodates investors with diverse financial capacities, including students, young professionals, retirees, and anyone seeking to grow their savings in a secure and accessible manner.

A STEPPING STONE TO OTHER INVESTMENTS

The money market serves as an excellent stepping stone for many investors, providing a solid foundation and essential experience that paves the way for exploring other diverse and potentially more rewarding investment avenues. As you embark on your journey to build wealth and secure your financial future, starting with money market investments can prove to be a strategic and empowering choice.

Building Financial Confidence: For novice investors, the money market offers a gentle introduction to the world of finance. With its low-risk nature and predictable returns, money market investments instill a sense of confidence and security, especially for those who are cautious about market volatility and uncertainty. As you witness your capital preserved and grow modestly in the money market, you gain the reassurance and knowledge necessary to venture into other investment options.

Understanding Financial Markets: Engaging with money market investments exposes you to key concepts and principles in financial markets. You begin to familiarize yourself with factors like interest rates, credit ratings, and the impact of economic indicators on investments. This foundational understanding forms a strong basis for comprehending more complex investment vehicles as you progress in your financial journey.

Growing Financial Savvy: Engaging in money market investments fosters a sense of financial literacy and savvy. As you track your investments, monitor market conditions, and stay informed about economic developments, you develop a keen awareness of financial news and trends. This growing financial intelligence arms you with the knowledge needed to make informed decisions in various investment domains.

Long-Term Investment Mindset: The money market encourages a long-term investment mindset. While money market investments offer short maturities, the principles of patience and discipline learned here can be carried forward to longer-term investment strategies. Gradually, you begin to recognize the value of staying committed to your financial goals and avoiding short-term market fluctuations.

3: DIFFERENCE BETWEEN MONEY MARKET AND OTHER INVESTMENT OPTIONS

In this chapter, we'll embark on a journey to explore the distinctive characteristics that set the money market apart from other investment options. Understanding these differences will empower you to make well-informed decisions about how to allocate your hard-earned funds.

Time Horizon: One of the most significant differences between the money market and other investment options lies in the time horizon. Money market instruments have short maturities, typically ranging from a few days to one year. In contrast, other investments, such as stocks and long-term bonds, have much longer time horizons, often extending to several years or even decades.

Risk Profile: Risk plays a crucial role in investment decisions. Money market investments are considered relatively safe due to their short-term nature and high credit quality. They offer a lower risk compared to other investment options, such as stocks, which can experience significant price fluctuations over the long term.

Return Expectations: While money market investments provide stability and liquidity, their return expectations are modest. Investors choose the money market primarily for capital preservation and ease of access to funds. In contrast, other investments, such as stocks and real estate, carry higher return potentials but also entail higher risk.

Market Volatility: The money market is characterized by low volatility, making it an appealing option for risk-averse investors seeking a steady and predictable income. On the other hand, other investments, especially in the stock market, are subject to market fluctuations that can lead to significant short-term gains or losses.

Investment Vehicles: Money market investments are primarily executed through short-term debt instruments, such as Treasury Bills, Certificates of Deposit, and Commercial Paper. Conversely, other investment options encompass a broad spectrum of assets, including stocks, bonds, real estate, mutual funds, exchange-traded funds (ETFs), and more.

Investment Objectives: Different investment options serve diverse objectives. The main objective of the money market is cash flow and is suitable for short-term goals, emergency funds, or preserving capital. Other investments are often pursued to achieve long-term growth, build wealth, and prepare for retirement.

Income vs. Growth: Money market investments primarily focus on generating income through interest payments. In contrast, other investments, particularly stocks, offer potential for capital appreciation and growth, in addition to dividend income.

Regulatory Environment: The money market is subject to strict regulations to maintain stability and protect investors. Government agencies, such as the Securities and Exchange Commission (SEC) in the United States, oversee various investment options to ensure transparency and fair practices.

Risk-Return Tradeoff: Investors often navigate the tradeoff between risk and return when making investment decisions. The money market prioritizes lower risk and stable returns, while other investment options may offer higher returns but come with higher inherent risks.

Investor Profile: The choice between money market and other investment options depends on individual investor profiles, risk tolerance, and financial goals. Conservative investors seeking short-term stability and liquidity may gravitate towards the money market, whereas those with a long-term horizon and higher risk tolerance may opt for other investments to capitalize on growth potential.

By recognizing the distinctions between the money market and other investment options, you gain valuable insights to construct a well-balanced investment portfolio tailored to your unique financial aspirations. As we venture further into the world of money market instruments, keep these distinctions in mind, and let them guide you toward sound investment choices.

PART 2: TYPES OF MONEY MARKET INSTRUMENTS

4: TREASURY BILLS (T-BILLS)

Treasury Bills (T-Bills) is a cornerstone of the money market. In this chapter, we will explore the ins and outs of T-Bills, understanding what they are, how they work, and why they are a popular choice for both individual and institutional investors seeking safety and liquidity.

Definition of Treasury Bills: Treasury Bills, commonly known as T-Bills, are discounted short-term debt securities issued by the government to raise funds to finance various activities and operations. When you invest in T-Bills, you are essentially lending money to the government at a discounted price (lower than the face value) with the promise of receiving the full face value at the end of the T-Bill's term. The difference between the discounted price (purchase price) and the face value represents the interest earned on the investment.

Maturity Periods: T-Bills come in different maturity periods, ranging from a few days to 52 weeks (1 year). The shorter the maturity, the lower the interest rate tends to be, as investors are willing to accept lower returns for the added liquidity and safety of shorter terms.

Example: Investor A purchases a 6-month T-Bill with a face value of $10,000 and a discount rate of 2%.

Discount Amount = Face Value x Discount Rate = $10,000 x 0.02 x (6/12) = $100

Purchase Price = Face Value - Discount Amount = $10,000 - $100 = $9,900

On the maturity date, which is 6 months after the issuance, the T-Bill reaches its full face value. Investor A receives $10,000.

How T-Bills are Issued and Sold: The U.S. Department of the Treasury conducts regular auctions to issue new T-Bills. These auctions are open to the public, financial institutions, and other entities. Investors place bids specifying the amount they want to invest and the interest rate they are willing to accept. The Treasury accepts the bids starting from the lowest interest rate until the total amount of T-Bills offered is fully allocated.

Competitive and Non-Competitive Bidding: Investors can participate in T-Bill auctions through either competitive or non-competitive bidding. In competitive bidding, investors specify the interest rate they desire, and if their bid is accepted, they receive the T-Bills at their proposed rate. In non-competitive bidding, investors agree to accept the interest rate determined by the auction and are guaranteed to receive the T-Bills.

Zero-Coupon Nature: T-Bills are known as zero-coupon securities because they do not pay periodic interest like traditional bonds. Instead, the difference between the purchase price and the face value at maturity represents the investor's earnings.

Government Backing: T-Bills are considered one of the safest investments available because they are backed by the full faith and credit of the government. This means that the U.S. government guarantees the timely payment of both the principal amount and interest.

Secondary Market Trading: Secondary market platforms for Treasury Bills (T-Bills) facilitate the buying and selling of these short-term government securities among investors after their initial issuance. These platforms provide liquidity and enable investors to exit or enter positions before the T-Bills reach maturity. Some examples of secondary market platforms for T-Bills include: Over-The-Counter (OTC) Markets, Broker-Dealer Platforms, Electronic Trading Platforms, Bond Exchanges, Money Market Funds, Government Securities Dealers and Interbank Markets.

T-Bills and Your Portfolio: T-Bills are a valuable addition to any investment portfolio. They provide a safe haven during times of market volatility and economic uncertainty. Conservative investors often use T-Bills as a way to preserve capital while earning a competitive return.

Tax Considerations: While interest earned from T-Bills is exempt from state and local taxes, it is subject to federal income tax. However, investors can defer paying taxes on the interest until the T-Bill matures, allowing for potential tax planning strategies.

Investing in T-Bills: Investing in T-Bills can be done directly through the TreasuryDirect website (www.treasurydirect.gov), or indirectly through financial institutions and brokers who offer T-Bills to their clients.

Treasury Bills offer an essential entry point into the world of money market investing, providing unparalleled safety and liquidity. As you explore this investment option, keep in mind that T-Bills are just one piece of the money market puzzle. In the following chapters, we'll continue our exploration of various money market instruments, empowering you to make confident investment decisions aligned with your financial goals.

5: CERTIFICATES OF DEPOSIT (CDS)

Certificates of Deposit (CDs), is a popular choice for investors seeking steady returns and the assurance of capital preservation. In this chapter, we'll delve into the ins and outs of CDs, understanding how they work, their benefits, and considerations for adding them to your investment portfolio.

Definition of Certificates of Deposit: Certificates of Deposit, commonly known as CDs, are time deposits offered by banks and credit unions to investors. When you purchase a CD, you are essentially lending money to the financial institution for a fixed period, known as the term or maturity, in exchange for a specified interest rate.

Maturity Periods: CDs come with various maturity periods, ranging from a few months to several years. The length of the term determines the interest rate, with longer terms generally offering higher rates.

Example: Investor B decides to invest $5,000 in a 1-year CD with a fixed interest rate of 2.5%. After 1 year (the maturity date), the CD reaches its full term.

Interest Earned = Principal Amount x Interest Rate = $5,000 x 0.025 = $125

Investor B is entitled to receive the principal amount of $5,000 and the interest earned of $125, totaling $5,125.

Fixed Interest Rates: Unlike other investments that may experience fluctuations in interest rates, CDs offer fixed interest rates for the entire duration of the term. This provides predictability and allows investors to know exactly how much they will earn at the end of the CD's term.

Early Withdrawal Penalties: Once you invest in a CD, your money is locked in for the agreed-upon term. If you withdraw funds before the CD's maturity, you may incur early withdrawal penalties, which can result in a loss of interest earnings or even a portion of the principal.

FDIC Insurance: CDs offered by banks are typically insured by the Federal Deposit Insurance Corporation (FDIC) in the United States. This means that even if the bank faces financial difficulties, your CD investment is protected up to the maximum coverage limit (currently $250,000 per depositor per institution).

Callable CDs: Some CDs are callable, meaning the bank has the option to "call back" the CD before its maturity date. Callable CDs often offer higher interest rates but come with the risk that the bank may redeem the CD early, potentially affecting your investment strategy.

CD Laddering: CD laddering is a strategy in which an investor spreads their funds across multiple CDs with different maturity dates. This approach allows for regular access to funds, takes advantage of different interest rate environments, and maintains a balance between liquidity and returns.

Advantages of CDs: CDs offer several advantages, including a higher interest rate than traditional savings accounts, low risk, FDIC insurance, and fixed returns. They are an attractive option for those looking to preserve capital while earning a reliable income.

CD vs. Money Market Fund: While both CDs and money market funds are considered safe investments, they have differences worth considering. CDs offer fixed interest rates and locked-in terms, while money market funds may have variable returns based on market conditions.

Choosing the Right CD: When selecting a CD, consider factors such as the term, interest rate, and financial institution. Shopping around for the best CD rates and terms can help you maximize your returns.

Certificates of Deposit present a compelling option for investors seeking a conservative approach to money market investing. Their fixed returns, FDIC insurance, and flexibility for various time horizons make them a valuable addition to any diversified investment portfolio.

6: COMMERCIAL PAPER

ommercial Paper is a vital instrument in the money market that fuels the short-term funding needs of corporations and financial institutions. In this chapter, we'll explore the world of Commercial Paper, understanding its purpose,
features, and significance in the financial landscape.

Definition of Commercial Paper: Commercial Paper (CP) represents unsecured, short-term debt instruments issued by corporations, financial institutions, and other large entities. These
entities use CP to raise funds quickly to meet immediate cash requirements, such as funding payroll, covering accounts payable,
or financing short-term projects.

Essentially, CP serves as a cost-effective way for these entities to
borrow from the investing public at a lower interest rate than
borrowing from banks. By accessing funds through the issuance
of discounted Commercial Paper, these entities can reduce their
operating costs and efficiently manage their short-term financing
needs.

Short Maturities: Commercial Paper typically matures in a range
of 1 to 270 days, making it a key player in the short-term financing
arena. The short maturity period provides issuers with flexibility,
and investors benefit from the potential to access funds promptly.

High Credit Quality: Commercial Paper is well-regarded for its
credit quality. Issuers with excellent credit ratings often tap into
the CP market, making it a relatively safe investment option for

buyers. However, investors should still assess credit ratings and creditworthiness before making investment decisions.

Issuers of Commercial Paper: The issuers of Commercial Paper vary widely, ranging from large corporations and financial institutions to municipalities and government-sponsored enterprises. These entities utilize CP to cover temporary funding needs and manage liquidity efficiently.

Commercial Paper Dealers: Commercial Paper is primarily sold through a network of dealers, including large banks and securities firms. Dealers play a crucial role in facilitating transactions, connecting issuers with investors, and providing liquidity to the CP market.

Discounted Purchase Price: Commercial Paper is typically sold at a discounted price from its face value, allowing investors to earn interest on the difference between the purchase price and the face value upon maturity. The difference represents the return on investment.

Example: Company XYZ decides to issue Commercial Paper to raise the needed funds. They issue a 90-day CP with a face value of $100,000 and an interest rate of 2.5%. Investor C purchases $100,000 worth of Company XYZ's 90-day Commercial Paper and holds the Commercial Paper for the entire 90-day term.

Discount Amount = Face Value x Discount Rate = $100,000 x 0.025 x (90/360) = $625

Issuance Price = Face Value - Discount Amount = $100,000 - $625 = $99,375

On the maturity date, which is 90 days after the issuance, the Commercial Paper reaches its full face value. Investor C receives $100,000 from the issuer.

Types of Commercial Paper: There are two main types of Commercial Paper: "Prime" and "Asset-Backed." Prime CP is issued by corporations with excellent credit ratings, while Asset-Backed CP is backed by specific assets, such as mortgages, auto loans, or credit card receivables.

Secondary Market Trading: While Commercial Paper is a primary market instrument, it can also be traded in the secondary market, same as Treasury Bills (listed previously). Secondary market trading allows investors to buy and sell CP before its maturity, providing added liquidity to this short-term investment.

Commercial Paper and Investors: Commercial Paper appeals to investors seeking a safe, short-term investment option with potentially higher returns than traditional savings accounts. It offers an opportunity to diversify portfolios and capture competitive yields with relatively low risk.

Risks of Commercial Paper: Although Commercial Paper is considered relatively safe due to high credit quality, it is not entirely risk-free. Credit risk remains a concern, and investors should carefully assess the creditworthiness of issuers to mitigate potential risks.

Commercial Paper serves as a crucial link in the money market chain, supporting the financial needs of corporations and offering investors a gateway to short-term, low-risk investments. As you continue your exploration of money market instruments, Commercial Paper presents a compelling choice to consider as part of a well-balanced investment portfolio.

7: REPURCHASE AGREEMENTS (REPOS)

Repurchase Agreements, commonly known as Repos, a vital component of the money market that facilitates short-term borrowing and lending between financial institutions. In this chapter, we'll delve into the mechanics of Repos, understanding their purpose, how they work, and their significance in the financial landscape.

Definition of Repurchase Agreements (Repos): A Repurchase Agreement (Repo) is a short-term financial transaction in which one party sells securities, typically government securities, to another party with an agreement to repurchase them at a later date, often the following day or within a few days. Repos act as collateralized loans with the securities serving as collateral for the cash loan.

Example: Party A (Borrower) has a need for short-term funds, while Party B (Lender) has excess cash and is willing to lend it out. Party A approaches Party B to enter into a repurchase agreement.

Party A sells a specific security (e.g., government bonds or Treasury Bills) to Party B at an agreed-upon price, say $100,000. This transaction is often referred to as the "repo" leg or the initial leg of the repurchase agreement.

Simultaneously, both parties agree that Party A will repurchase the same security from Party B for $100,500 in one week. At the end of the one-week period, Party A repurchases the security from Party B at the agreed-upon repurchase price, which is $100,500 (including interest).

The interest earned by Party B in this example is $500 ($100,500 - $100,000). This $500 represents the compensation to Party B for lending their funds to Party A for the one-week period.

Two Parties Involved: In a Repo, there are two parties involved: the party selling the securities (the "seller" or "borrower") and the party purchasing the securities (the "buyer" or "lender"). The seller borrows cash by selling the securities, while the buyer provides the cash in exchange for the securities with the expectation of receiving them back, plus interest, at the agreed-upon repurchase date.

Interest Rate (Repo Rate): The difference between the original sale price and the repurchase price represents the interest earned by the buyer. This interest rate is known as the "Repo Rate" and serves as the compensation for the lender's temporary use of funds. In the above example, the Repo Rate is $500/$100,000 x 100 = 0.5%

Collateralization: Repos are considered safe investments because they are collateralized with high-quality securities, typically government securities, such as Treasury Bills or Treasury Bonds. In case the seller defaults on repurchasing the securities, the buyer can sell the collateral to recover their funds.

Term Length: Repo transactions come with varying term lengths, often ranging from overnight (an "overnight repo") to several days or weeks. The term is agreed upon by both parties before the transaction takes place.

Role in Money Market Liquidity: Repos play a critical role in providing short-term liquidity to financial institutions, allowing them to meet reserve requirements and manage their short-term funding needs efficiently.

Reverse Repos: A reverse Repo is the opposite of a Repo transaction. In a reverse Repo, the financial institution acts as the buyer, lending cash to another party against the collateral of government securities. Reverse Repos serve as a tool for the central bank to manage monetary policy and control the money supply.

Role in Central Bank Operations: Central banks, such as the Federal Reserve in the United States, use Repos as a tool for implementing monetary policy. By conducting Repos or reverse Repos with financial institutions, central banks can influence interest rates, manage liquidity in the banking system, and achieve their policy objectives.

Advantages and Risks of Repos: For investors, Repos offer a safe and short-term investment option with potential returns. However, as with any investment, there are risks involved, such as the potential for fluctuations in interest rates and counterparty risks.

Participation in Repos: While Repos are typically conducted between financial institutions, individual investors can participate indirectly through money market funds that invest in Repos or government securities.

Repurchase Agreements are an integral part of the money market, providing essential short-term funding and liquidity management solutions for financial institutions. Understanding Repos allows investors to appreciate the intricacies of this market and explore its potential benefits as part of a diversified investment strategy.

8: MONEY MARKET FUNDS

Money Market Funds are a popular investment option that offers convenience, diversification, and stability for investors seeking a safe place to park their cash. In this chapter, we'll explore the mechanics of Money Market Funds, their benefits, and how they play a vital role in the money market ecosystem.

Definition of Money Market Funds: Money Market Funds (MMFs) are mutual funds that invest in short-term, low-risk money market instruments. These funds pool money from multiple investors and allocate it to a diversified portfolio of money market securities, aiming to preserve capital and provide a modest level of income.

Investment Holdings: Money Market Funds invest in a range of money market instruments, such as Treasury Bills, Certificates of Deposit, Commercial Paper, Repurchase Agreements, and short-term government and corporate debt. The fund manager carefully selects these instruments to achieve the fund's investment objectives.

Stable Net Asset Value (NAV): One key feature of Money Market Funds is that they typically maintain a stable Net Asset Value (NAV) of $1 per share. So, whenever investors buy or sell shares, they get or pay $1 for each share, ensuring a steady price with minimal changes..

Liquidity and Accessibility: Money Market Funds offer high liquidity, allowing investors to buy or sell shares on any business day. The ease of access to funds makes them a popular choice for individuals and institutions seeking quick and hassle-free cash management.

Regulatory Oversight: Money Market Funds are subject to strict regulatory guidelines to ensure their safety and stability. In the United States, the Securities and Exchange Commission (SEC) regulates MMFs, requiring them to meet specific portfolio requirements and maintain sufficient liquidity to meet redemptions.

Treasury Money Market Funds: Some Money Market Funds focus exclusively on investing in U.S. Treasury and government-related securities. These funds are often considered among the safest, given their backing by the U.S. government.

Tax Considerations: In many countries, the interest income earned from Money Market Funds is subject to taxation at the individual's applicable tax rate. Tax-advantaged accounts, such as Individual Retirement Accounts (IRAs) in the United States, offer potential tax benefits when holding MMFs.

Institutional vs. Retail Money Market Funds: Money Market Funds can be classified as institutional or retail based on the type of investors they cater to. Institutional funds typically have higher minimum investment requirements and lower expense ratios, attracting large investors like corporations and institutional investors.

Role in the Money Market: Money Market Funds play a significant role in providing short-term financing to governments and corporations by investing in money market instruments. They also contribute to maintaining stability in the financial system through their conservative investment approach.

Risks and Considerations: While Money Market Funds are considered low-risk, they are not entirely immune to risks. Investors should be aware of factors like interest rate fluctuations, credit risks, and the potential for a fund's NAV to "break the buck," although this is a rare occurrence.

Money Market Funds offer an attractive blend of safety, liquidity, and convenience, making them an excellent choice for those seeking stable short-term investments. As you explore the options available in the money market, Money Market Funds stand as a reliable tool for cash management and preserving capital.

9: MUNICIPAL NOTES

Municipal Notes are an essential component of the money market that provides state and local governments with a means to raise short-term funds for various public projects and expenses. In this chapter, we'll explore the intricacies of Municipal Notes, their unique features, and the benefits they offer to both issuers and investors.

Definition of Municipal Notes: Municipal Notes, often referred to as "Muni Notes" or "Tax Anticipation Notes (TANs)," are short-term debt securities issued by state and local governments, as well as municipal entities such as school districts or public utilities. These notes serve as a temporary funding solution to cover capital expenditures or bridge budget gaps until long-term financing can be arranged.

Short Maturity Period: Municipal Notes have relatively short maturities, typically ranging from a few months to a year. The short-term nature aligns with the cash flow needs of the issuing government, allowing them to meet their financial obligations promptly.

Example: City X decides to issue Municipal Notes to raise the needed funds. They issue a 6-month Municipal Note with a face value of $50,000 and a coupon rate of 3%. At the end of the 6-month term (the maturity date), the Municipal Note reaches its full term.

Interest Earned = Principal Amount x Interest Rate

$$= \$50,000 \times 0.03 \times (180/360) = \$750$$

City X repays the face value of $50,000 to Investor D along with the interest earned of $750 (total of $50,750).

Purpose of Issuance: Governments issue Municipal Notes for various purposes, such as funding infrastructure projects, covering operating expenses, and managing cash flow fluctuations. These notes play a crucial role in financing essential public services and projects.

Tax Benefits: One significant advantage of investing in Municipal Notes is the potential for tax-exempt income. Interest earned from Municipal Notes issued by local governments within the investor's state is often exempt from federal income tax. In some cases, interest may also be exempt from state and local taxes, making Municipal Notes an attractive choice for investors in higher tax brackets.

Types of Municipal Notes: There are several types of Municipal Notes, each tailored to specific financing needs. Some common types include Tax Anticipation Notes (TANs), Revenue Anticipation Notes (RANs), Bond Anticipation Notes (BANs), and Construction Loan Notes (CLNs).

Credit Ratings: The creditworthiness of Municipal Notes varies based on the issuing government's financial stability and ability to repay the debt. To assess risk, investors rely on credit ratings assigned by rating agencies, such as Standard & Poor's, Moody's, or Fitch.

Role in the Money Market: Municipal Notes contribute to the money market's liquidity by offering short-term investment opportunities to individuals, corporations, and institutions. They provide investors with a safe option to park funds temporarily while earning competitive returns.

Secondary Market Trading: While Municipal Notes are primarily held until maturity, they can be traded in the secondary market before their term expires. Secondary market trading allows investors to buy and sell Municipal Notes, enhancing their liquidity.

Risks and Considerations: While Municipal Notes are generally considered low-risk, there are factors to be aware of. Investors should carefully evaluate the creditworthiness of the issuing government and assess any potential changes in economic conditions or local fiscal policies that could impact repayment.

Local Impact: Investing in Municipal Notes allows individuals to support local communities and public projects directly. The funds raised from Municipal Note issuance often contribute to the betterment of local infrastructure, schools, public services, and other essential initiatives.

Municipal Notes play a critical role in supporting the financial needs of state and local governments while offering investors a tax-advantaged short-term investment option. As you explore the diverse landscape of the money market, Municipal Notes stand as a valuable addition to consider in building a well-rounded and socially impactful investment portfolio.

10: BANKER'S ACCEPTANCES (BAS)

Banker's Acceptances are a unique and widely used financial instrument in international trade and commerce. In this chapter, we'll explore the intricacies of Banker's Acceptances, understanding their purpose, how they work, and their significance in facilitating secure and efficient cross-border transactions.

Definition of Banker's Acceptances: Banker's Acceptances (BAs) are time drafts or short-term promissory notes issued by a bank on behalf of its customers. These financial instruments serve as a guarantee of payment for goods and services in international trade transactions. BAs are widely used to facilitate secure trade between importers and exporters.

International Trade Transactions: Banker's Acceptances are especially prevalent in international trade scenarios, where trust and credibility play a vital role. Exporters request BAs from the importer's bank, ensuring that the payment for the goods will be made at a specified future date.

Process of Issuance: In a typical Banker's Acceptance transaction, an exporter presents the draft or promissory note to their bank, instructing the bank to issue a BA. The bank accepts the draft, indicating its commitment to pay the specified amount at the maturity date. The exporter can then present the BA to a buyer, who can accept it, signaling their commitment to pay the amount on the maturity date.

Maturity Period: Banker's Acceptances typically have short maturities, ranging from a few weeks to several months. The maturity period is agreed upon at the time of issuance and is based on the specific trade transaction's timeline.

Example: Company Y, an importer, purchases a large shipment of goods from an overseas supplier. The overseas supplier requires payment upfront or a guarantee of payment from a reputable bank before shipping the goods. Company Y approaches its bank for a Banker's Acceptances (BA) to facilitate the transaction. Company Y provides all the necessary documentation. The bank is satisfied with the creditworthiness of Company Y and the overseas supplier, and issues a 90-day BA in favor of the supplier.

The Bank offers 90-day BA with a face value of $100,000 and a discount rate of 2% to Investor D. Investor D buys the BA and holds it for the entire term of 90 days.

Discount Amount = Face Value x Discount Rate = = $100,000 x 0.02 x (90/360) = $500

Issuance Price = Face Value - Discount Amount = $100,000 - $500 = $99,500

On the maturity date, Investor E presents the BA to the bank for payment of $100,000.

Creditworthiness and Endorsement: The creditworthiness of the issuing bank is crucial in Banker's Acceptances. Exporters and buyers often look for BAs from reputable banks with high credit ratings. Additionally, BAs can be endorsed and traded, allowing the holder to transfer the right to receive payment to another party.

Secondary Market Trading: Banker's Acceptances can be traded in the secondary market before their maturity, providing liquidity to investors who may need to access funds before the BA's payment date.

Role in Facilitating Trade: Banker's Acceptances play a pivotal role in international trade finance, providing a secure mechanism for exporters to receive payment and importers to ensure the delivery and quality of goods.

Commercial vs. Financial Banker's Acceptances: There are two main types of Banker's Acceptances: commercial BAs and financial BAs. Commercial BAs are used in trade transactions, while financial BAs are related to financial transactions, such as short-term borrowing and lending between banks.

Regulated by Banking Authorities: Banker's Acceptances are subject to regulation and oversight by banking authorities in the countries where they are issued. These regulations ensure their proper use and adherence to banking standards.

Global Impact: The use of Banker's Acceptances facilitates smoother and more reliable international trade, promoting economic growth, and strengthening commercial relationships between countries.

Banker's Acceptances serve as a bridge between international trade partners, instilling confidence and trust in cross-border transactions. Understanding the role of BAs will broaden your understanding of the global financial system and the mechanisms that underpin international trade.

11: EURODOLLARS

E urodollars are a significant component of the global financial system that plays a crucial role in international trade and finance. In this chapter, we'll explore the intricacies of Eurodollars, understanding their origin, how they function, and their significance in facilitating cross-border transactions and investments.

Definition of Eurodollars: Eurodollars are U.S. dollars held in banks located outside the United States. Contrary to what the name might suggest, Eurodollars have no direct connection to the European currency "Euro" but rather emerged in the 1950s as U.S. dollars held in European banks.

Origin of Eurodollars: Eurodollars originated as a result of the post-World War II economic landscape. During this period, European banks held U.S. dollars to facilitate international trade and investment, and these deposits became known as Eurodollars.

Offshore Financial Centers: Eurodollars are often held in offshore financial centers, such as London, Luxembourg, or the Cayman Islands, where banks offer financial services to international clients.

Role in International Trade and Finance: Eurodollars play a vital role in international trade and finance as they serve as a medium for cross-border transactions and investments. They facilitate global business activities, acting as a key funding source for multinational corporations and financial institutions.

Maturity Period: Eurodollars do not have a standardized or fixed maturity period like traditional bonds or certificates of deposit (CDs). Eurodollar deposits are negotiated between the depositor and the bank, allowing for flexibility in determining the maturity period. The depositor and the bank can agree on a specific maturity date that aligns with the depositor's needs, ranging from overnight to several months.

Example: Investor F decides to invest $30,000 in Eurodollars. Investor F negotiates the terms of the Eurodollar deposit with the bank and agree on a deposit term of 3 months and a fixed interest rate of 2%. At the end of the 3-month deposit term, the Eurodollar deposit matures.

Interest Earned = Principal Amount x Interest Rate = $30,000 x 0.02 x (90/360) = $150

The Bank pays Investor F the principal amount of $25,000 and the interest earned of $150, totaling $25,150.

Attraction for Investors: Eurodollars are attractive to investors due to their high liquidity, flexibility, and potential for higher returns compared to domestic U.S. dollar accounts. They are often used by investors seeking a safe haven for their funds or looking to take advantage of favorable interest rate differentials.

Eurodollar Market and LIBOR: The Eurodollar market is a vast and active market for trading Eurodollar-denominated deposits. It is closely linked to the London Interbank Offered Rate (LIBOR), which serves as a benchmark for short-term interest rates in the Eurodollar market.

Currency Exchange Risks: Although Eurodollars are denominated in U.S. dollars, they still carry currency exchange risks for investors who convert other currencies to U.S. dollars to invest in Eurodollars. For non US residents, investing in Eurodollars is a powerful tool as a hedge against inflation and currency fluctuations, if your national currency is much weaker compared to the dollar.

Regulatory Considerations: Eurodollars are subject to the banking regulations of the countries in which they are held. The lack of direct oversight by U.S. regulatory authorities can present challenges and risks for investors.

Impact on Monetary Policy: The large volume of Eurodollars held outside the U.S. can influence the effectiveness of U.S. monetary policy, as these funds may flow in or out of the U.S. based on changes in interest rates and market conditions.

Cross-Border Capital Flows: The Eurodollar market reflects the dynamic nature of cross-border capital flows, acting as a barometer for global economic conditions and financial market sentiment.

Eurodollars remain a significant force in the global financial landscape, underpinning international trade and investment activities. Understanding the role of Eurodollars in will enhance your grasp of the interconnectedness of the global economy and its role in your financial portfolio.

12: FLOATING RATE NOTES (FRNS)

Floating Rate Notes (FRNs) is a unique type of bond that offers investors protection against interest rate fluctuations. In this chapter, we'll explore the intricacies of Floating Rate Notes, understanding how they work, their benefits, and their significance in a changing interest rate environment.

Definition of Floating Rate Notes: Floating Rate Notes, commonly known as FRNs, are debt securities issued by governments, corporations, or other entities. Unlike traditional fixed-rate bonds, the interest rate on FRNs adjusts periodically based on a reference or benchmark interest rate, such as the London Interbank Offered Rate (LIBOR), the U.S. Treasury Bill rate or other market-determined reference rates.

Adjustable Interest Rates: The key feature of FRNs is their adjustable interest rates. Typically, the interest rate is set as a spread (or margin) above or below the reference rate. For example, an FRN might be issued with an interest rate equal to LIBOR plus 0.50%. As LIBOR changes, the interest rate on the FRN will change accordingly.

Protection Against Interest Rate Risk: FRNs offer investors protection against interest rate risk, as their interest payments adjust with changes in the reference rate. When interest rates rise, the interest paid on FRNs increases, providing investors with higher income. Conversely, when interest rates fall, the interest paid on FRNs decreases.

Maturity Periods and Terms: Floating Rate Notes come with various maturity periods, ranging from short-term to long-term. The terms are set at the time of issuance, and investors can choose FRNs with maturity dates that align with their investment objectives. Here are some examples of common maturity periods for FRNs:

- Short-term FRNs: These have maturity periods ranging from 6 months to 2 years.

- Medium-term FRNs: These have maturity periods ranging from 2 years to 5 years.

- Long-term FRNs: These have maturity periods exceeding 5 years.

Interest Rate Reset Periods: The interest rate on FRNs resets at specific intervals, such as quarterly, semi-annually, or annually. The frequency of the reset period is specified in the bond's terms.

- Quarterly Adjustment: The interest rate on the FRN adjusts every quarter based on the prevailing benchmark rate.

- Semi-Annual Adjustment: The interest rate adjusts twice a year, typically at six-month intervals.

- Annual Adjustment: The interest rate adjusts once a year, usually on the anniversary of the FRN issuance.

Example: Company X decides to issue a $50 million FRN through an investment bank to fund their expansion project. Company X and the investment bank agrees to the following terms:

- Maturity Period: 1 year

- Benchmark Rate: 6-month LIBOR

- Spread: +1.25% above the 6-month LIBOR

- Interest Rate Adjustment Frequency: Quarterly

- Coupon Payment: Quarterly

Investor G decides to subscribe to this offer and invest $20,000 at the current 6-month LIBOR of 2%. At the first coupon payment at 90 days.

Interest Rate = Benchmark Rate + Spread = 2% + 1.25% = 3.25%

Interest Earned = Principal Amount x Interest Rate

$$= \$20,000 \times 0.0325 \times (90/360) = \$162.50$$

Investor G receives $162.50 as coupon payment. The interest rate is now adjusted to reflect the current 6-month LIBOR of 2.1%.

Interest Rate = Benchmark Rate + Spread = 2.1% + 1.25% = 3.35%

Interest Earned = Principal Amount x Interest Rate

$$= \$20,000 \times 0.0335 \times (90/360) = \$167.50$$

Investor G receives $162.50 as coupon payment. The interest rate is now adjusted to reflect the current 6-month LIBOR of 2.1%.

Investor G receives $167.50 as coupon payment. The interest rate again adjusted and the process is repeated until the FRN matures in one year.

Liquidity and Secondary Market Trading: FRNs are actively traded in the secondary market, providing investors with liquidity and the ability to buy or sell their holdings before maturity.

Attraction for Investors: FRNs are attractive to investors seeking a hedge against interest rate risk, especially in environments where interest rates are expected to change significantly. They are also appealing for those who desire a regular stream of income that adjusts with prevailing market rates.

Issuers of Floating Rate Notes: Governments, corporations, and financial institutions are among the common issuers of FRNs. The entities issue FRNs to raise capital and manage their funding needs effectively.

Credit Considerations: As with any bond investment, credit considerations are crucial when investing in FRNs. Investors should assess the creditworthiness of the issuer to gauge the risk of default.

Diversification and Portfolio Balance: FRNs can serve as a valuable addition to a diversified investment portfolio, helping to balance the impact of interest rate fluctuations on fixed-income holdings.

Floating Rate Notes present an enticing option for investors seeking to mitigate interest rate risk and stay flexible in a changing market environment. Understanding the dynamics of FRNs will empower you to make informed decisions to optimize your investment strategy.

13: TREASURY MONEY MARKET MUTUAL FUNDS (TMMFS)

Treasury Money Market Mutual Funds (TMMFs) is a popular and accessible investment option for individuals and institutions seeking safety, liquidity, and competitive yields within the money market. In this chapter, we'll explore the intricacies of TMMFs, understanding their features, benefits, and considerations for investors.

Definition of Treasury Money Market Mutual Funds: Treasury Money Market Mutual Funds are mutual funds that primarily invest in short-term U.S. Treasury securities and other high-quality money market instruments. These funds pool money from multiple investors to create a diversified portfolio of low-risk, short-term securities.

Portfolio Composition: TMMFs invest in a variety of money market instruments, with a significant focus on Treasury Bills, Treasury Notes, and other government securities. The portfolio aims to provide stability, liquidity, and preservation of capital for investors.

Maturity Periods and Terms: Treasury Money Market Mutual Funds (TMMFs) are characterized by their short-term nature, typically offering maturity periods ranging from a few days to a few months. The terms of TMMFs are structured to align with investors' need for stability, safety, and accessibility to their funds.

Stability and Net Asset Value (NAV): TMMFs are designed to maintain a stable Net Asset Value (NAV) of $1 per share. This stability allows investors to redeem their shares at any time and receive the full value of their investment, plus any interest earned.

Low Risk and Credit Quality: TMMFs invest in high-quality, short-term securities, which are generally considered low risk. The emphasis on U.S. government securities ensures a high level of credit quality and minimizes the risk of default.

Liquidity and Accessibility: Treasury Money Market Mutual Funds offer high liquidity, allowing investors to buy or sell shares on any business day. This easy access to funds makes TMMFs a convenient option for cash management and emergency savings.

Attractive Yields: While TMMFs prioritize safety, they still aim to provide competitive yields relative to other money market instruments. The yields are influenced by prevailing interest rates and the types of securities in the fund's portfolio.

Dividends and Taxation: TMMFs pay dividends to investors based on the interest earned from their underlying investments. Dividends from TMMFs are generally taxable at the individual's applicable tax rate.

Regulatory Oversight: Treasury Money Market Mutual Funds are subject to regulation and oversight by the U.S. Securities and Exchange Commission (SEC) to ensure compliance with investment guidelines and protection of investors' interests.

Investment Minimums: TMMFs typically have low investment minimums, making them accessible to a wide range of investors, including individuals, corporations, and institutional investors.

Role in Cash Management: Treasury Money Market Mutual Funds are popular choices for cash management, short-term savings goals, and as a temporary parking place for funds awaiting future investment opportunities.

Treasury Money Market Mutual Funds offer a secure and convenient avenue for investors to participate in the money market while earning competitive returns on their short-term investments. Understanding TMMFs will empower you to make informed decisions in managing your funds efficiently and achieving your financial objectives.

14: TAX-EXEMPT COMMERCIAL PAPER

Tax-Exempt Commercial Paper is a specialized type of short-term debt instrument that provides issuers with a cost-effective way to raise capital while offering investors certain tax advantages. In this chapter, we'll explore the intricacies of Tax-Exempt Commercial Paper, understanding its features, benefits, and considerations for both issuers and investors.

Definition of Tax-Exempt Commercial Paper: Tax-Exempt Commercial Paper (TECP) refers to short-term debt securities issued by corporations, municipalities, and other entities to raise funds for a variety of short-term financing needs. What makes TECP unique is its tax-exempt status, meaning the interest earned by investors is typically exempt from federal income tax.

Maturity Periods: Tax-Exempt Commercial Paper generally has maturities ranging from a few days to up to 270 days. The short-term nature of TECP makes it a popular choice for issuers with short-term funding requirements.

Issuers of TECP: Both corporations and municipalities can issue Tax-Exempt Commercial Paper. Municipalities often use TECP to finance public projects and infrastructure initiatives, while corporations utilize TECP for working capital and operational needs.

Tax Benefits for Investors: The primary advantage of investing in Tax-Exempt Commercial Paper is the potential for tax savings.

Interest earned from TECP is typically exempt from federal income tax, making it an appealing option for investors in higher tax brackets.

Credit Considerations: As with any debt instrument, investors should assess the creditworthiness of the issuer before investing in Tax-Exempt Commercial Paper. Municipal issuers, in particular, may have varying credit profiles based on their financial health and revenue sources.

Interest Rates and Yields: The interest rates on Tax-Exempt Commercial Paper are generally lower than those on taxable commercial paper due to the tax benefits offered to investors. The yields on TECP may vary based on the credit quality of the issuer and prevailing market conditions.

Secondary Market Trading: While Tax-Exempt Commercial Paper can be held until maturity, it is often traded in the secondary market. Secondary market trading allows investors to buy and sell TECP before its maturity, providing liquidity and flexibility.

Role in Municipal Finance: Tax-Exempt Commercial Paper plays a vital role in municipal finance, offering municipalities a cost-effective way to raise short-term funds for public projects and operational needs.

Regulatory Oversight: Tax-Exempt Commercial Paper issuers must adhere to securities regulations and disclosure requirements to ensure transparency and investor protection.

Risks and Considerations: Investors should be aware that while Tax-Exempt Commercial Paper offers tax advantages, it still carries investment risks. Factors such as interest rate fluctuations, credit risks, and market conditions can impact the performance of TECP investments.

Tax-Exempt Commercial Paper presents an attractive opportunity for investors seeking short-term, tax-advantaged investment options while supporting municipal financing initiatives. Understanding the role of Tax-Exempt Commercial Paper will empower you to make informed decisions to optimize your investment strategy.

15: ASSET-BACKED COMMERCIAL PAPER (ABCP)

Asset-Backed Commercial Paper is a specialized form of short-term debt instrument that derives its value from underlying pools of assets. In this chapter, we'll explore the intricacies of Asset-Backed Commercial Paper, understanding its structure, benefits, and considerations for investors and issuers.

Definition of Asset-Backed Commercial Paper: Asset-Backed Commercial Paper (ABCP) is a type of short-term debt security that is backed by a pool of financial assets, such as loans, leases, or receivables. These assets serve as collateral, providing security to investors.

Special Purpose Vehicles (SPVs): To issue Asset-Backed Commercial Paper, issuers often create Special Purpose Vehicles (SPVs) to hold and manage the pool of assets. The SPV is a separate legal entity established solely for the purpose of issuing ABCP. The SPV issues short-term debt securities called Asset-Backed Commercial Paper (ABCP). These securities represent a proportionate interest in the pool of underlying financial assets.

Securitization Process: The process of creating Asset-Backed Commercial Paper involves securitization, where financial assets are pooled together, and the cash flows generated from those assets are used to make interest and principal payments to ABCP investors.

Sale to Investors: The ABCP is then offered to institutional investors, money market funds, corporations, and other eligible investors in the financial markets. These investors are attracted to ABCP due to its short-term nature, high credit quality, and potential for slightly higher yields compared to traditional money market instruments.

Investors purchase the ABCP at face value, which is usually $1,000 per unit, with maturity periods typically ranging from a few days to several months. Throughout the life of the ABCP, investors receive interest payments periodically based on the underlying cash flows generated by the pool of financial assets.

Maturity and Repayment: Asset-Backed Commercial Paper typically has maturities ranging from a few days to a few months. The short-term nature of ABCP makes it attractive to investors seeking liquidity and flexibility. As the ABCP reaches its maturity date, the investors are repaid the face value of their investment. The repayment is made using the cash flows generated by the underlying financial assets.

Credit Quality and Ratings: The credit quality of Asset-Backed Commercial Paper varies based on the underlying assets and the creditworthiness of the originator. Credit rating agencies assign ratings to ABCP based on their assessment of credit risk.

Diversification and Risk Mitigation: The pool of underlying assets in ABCP provides diversification, reducing the impact of default risk associated with individual assets. This diversification enhances the overall credit quality of the ABCP.

Yield and Returns: Asset-Backed Commercial Paper offers competitive yields compared to traditional money market instruments due to the potential credit enhancement from the underlying assets.

Secondary Market Trading: While ABCP is designed to be held until maturity, it can be traded in the secondary market. Secondary market trading offers investors the ability to buy and sell ABCP before its maturity date.

Role in Financing and Funding: Asset-Backed Commercial Paper serves as an important source of funding for companies and financial institutions, allowing them to convert illiquid assets into tradable securities.

Risks and Considerations: Investors in Asset-Backed Commercial Paper should carefully assess the underlying assets, the credit quality of the originator, and the structure of the securitization. Market conditions and changes in interest rates can also impact the performance of ABCP.

Asset-Backed Commercial Paper plays a significant role in the financial markets, offering investors an opportunity to participate in the short-term debt market while benefiting from underlying asset collateral. Understanding the dynamics of Asset-Backed Commercial Paper will empower you to make informed decisions in building a robust and diversified investment portfolio.

PART 3: INVESTING IN THE MONEY MARKET

16: ASSESSING RISK IN MONEY MARKET INVESTMENTS

Welcome to the critical aspect of money market investing—assessing risk. In this chapter, we'll explore the essential considerations for evaluating risk in money market investments, understanding the factors that influence risk levels, and learning how to make informed decisions to protect and optimize your investment portfolio.

Understanding Risk in Money Market Investments: Risk is an inherent part of investing, and money market investments are no exception. While money market instruments are generally considered low-risk, various factors can influence the level of risk associated with each investment.

Credit Risk: One of the primary risks in money market investments is credit risk. This refers to the likelihood that the issuer of the instrument may default on its financial obligations, resulting in potential losses for investors.

Credit Ratings: Credit ratings assigned by rating agencies offer valuable insights into the creditworthiness of issuers. Higher-rated instruments typically indicate lower credit risk, while lower-rated instruments may offer higher yields but come with increased credit risk.

Interest Rate Risk: Money market investments are subject to interest rate risk, especially fixed-rate instruments. Changes in interest rates can impact the value of these investments, causing fluctuations in prices and yields.

Market and Liquidity Risk: While money market instruments are generally highly liquid, some less-traded or specialized instruments may face liquidity risk. In times of market stress or economic downturns, liquidity may become a concern for certain investments.

Inflation Risk: Money market investments, especially those with fixed interest rates, may be exposed to inflation risk. Inflation erodes the purchasing power of future cash flows, potentially reducing the real value of returns.

Currency Risk (for international investments): If you invest in money market instruments denominated in foreign currencies, currency risk comes into play. Exchange rate fluctuations can impact the value of your investment when converting back to your home currency.

Diversification as Risk Mitigation: Diversification is a fundamental strategy to mitigate risk. By spreading your investments across various money market instruments, issuers, and sectors, you can reduce the impact of any single investment's poor performance.

Assessing Your Risk Tolerance: Understanding your risk tolerance is crucial. Conservative investors may prefer low-risk money market investments, while those with higher risk tolerance may consider slightly riskier options for potential higher returns.

Periodic Review and Monitoring: Risk assessment is an ongoing process. Periodically review your investments, assess market conditions, and stay informed about changes in credit ratings and economic indicators that may impact your money market holdings.

By mastering the art of assessing risk in money market investments, you can make prudent decisions that align with your financial goals and risk appetite. Risk is an integral part of the process, and thoughtful evaluation can lead to a well-balanced and resilient investment portfolio.

17: BUILDING A MONEY MARKET INVESTMENT STRATEGY

Building a money market investment strategy requires careful thought, research, and understanding of your financial objectives. In this chapter, we'll guide you through the process of creating a well-rounded and effective strategy to optimize your returns while managing risk. Let's explore the key steps to craft a successful money market investment approach.

Define Your Financial Goals: Start by defining your financial goals and objectives. Are you investing for short-term liquidity needs, saving for a specific goal, or seeking to preserve capital while earning a competitive return? Understanding your goals will help shape your investment strategy.

Assess Your Risk Tolerance: Understand your risk tolerance and comfort level with potential fluctuations in your investments. While money market instruments are generally low-risk, some options carry slightly higher risks for potentially higher returns. Determine what level of risk aligns with your financial goals.

Research Money Market Instruments: Familiarize yourself with the various money market instruments available, such as Treasury Bills, CDs, Money Market Funds, and short-term bonds. Each instrument has distinct characteristics, risk profiles, and potential returns.

Choose the Suitable Money Market Instruments: Select money market instruments that align with your financial goals, risk tolerance, and investment horizon. Consider factors such as credit quality, interest rates, and liquidity when choosing instruments.

Diversification for Stability: Embrace the power of diversification to spread risk across different money market instruments, issuers, and maturities. A well-diversified portfolio can help protect your investments from the impact of individual instrument performance.

Consider Time Horizon: Your time horizon is crucial in selecting suitable money market instruments. For short-term needs, opt for highly liquid and short-maturity instruments. For longer-term goals, explore options with slightly longer maturities for potentially higher returns.

Evaluate Credit Quality: Assess the credit quality of issuers if you are considering investing in corporate or municipal money market instruments. Higher credit quality offers more security but may come with slightly lower yields.

Understand Fees and Expenses: Be mindful of fees and expenses associated with money market instruments, especially Money Market Funds. Lower expenses can contribute to better net returns.

Monitor Interest Rates: Stay informed about changes in interest rates and market conditions. Adjust your strategy accordingly to take advantage of potential rate increases or protect against rate decreases.

Rebalance Periodically: Periodically review your money market investment portfolio and rebalance as needed to maintain your desired asset allocation. Rebalancing ensures that your investments align with your original strategy.

Stay Informed and Seek Professional Advice: Continuously educate yourself about money market investments and financial markets. If needed, seek guidance from a financial advisor to tailor your strategy to your specific financial situation and goals.

By considering your risk tolerance, diversifying your investments, and staying informed, you can create a well-structured plan that aligns with your financial aspirations. Investment decisions should be based on your unique circumstances and goals.

18: HOW TO INVEST IN MONEY MARKET INSTRUMENTS

Investing in money market instruments is a straightforward process that offers individuals and institutions the opportunity to preserve capital, earn competitive yields, and maintain liquidity. In this chapter, we will guide you through the essential steps to get started with investing in money market instruments. Whether you are looking for a safe haven for your cash reserves or seeking short-term, low-risk opportunities, understanding how to invest in money market instruments will empower you to make informed decisions aligned with your financial goals.

OPENING A MONEY MARKET ACCOUNT

The first step to invest in money market instruments is to open a money market account. Most financial institutions, such as banks and credit unions, offer money market accounts that provide easy access to money market instruments. These accounts may include Treasury bills (T-Bills), Certificates of Deposit (CDs), and other money market instruments.

WORKING WITH A BROKER OR FINANCIAL ADVISOR

If you prefer a more hands-on approach or have specific investment preferences, consider working with a broker or financial advisor. They can assist you in selecting the most suitable money market instruments based on your financial situation, risk tolerance, and investment objectives. Financial professionals can also provide valuable insights into current market conditions and help you build a diversified money market portfolio.

DIRECT INVESTING VS. MONEY MARKET FUNDS

When investing in money market instruments, you have two primary options: direct investing or money market funds. Direct investing involves purchasing individual money market instruments, such as T-Bills or CDs, directly from the issuing institution. On the other hand, money market funds pool money from multiple investors to invest in a diversified portfolio of money market instruments. Money market funds offer convenience and instant diversification, making them an attractive choice for many investors.

EVALUATING INVESTMENT COSTS AND EXPENSES

Before investing, carefully assess the costs and expenses associated with money market instruments. While money market investments are generally low-risk, it's essential to understand any fees or commissions charged by brokers or financial institutions. For money market funds, evaluate expense ratios, which represent the percentage of fund assets used to cover operating expenses. Lower expense ratios can have a positive impact on your overall returns.

PLACE YOUR INVESTMENT ORDER

Once you've carefully evaluated the various money market instruments or funds and have decided on your investment strategy, it's time to take action and place your investment order. This step involves executing the decision you've made and committing your funds to the chosen money market investment.

Fund Your Investment Account: Ensure that you have an active investment account with the financial institution or brokerage firm through which you plan to invest in money market instruments and that you have adequate funds to cover the transaction.

Investment Amount and Duration: Determine the amount you wish to invest in the money market instrument or fund. For example, if you opt for Treasury bills, specify the face value of the T-Bill (e.g., $1,000) you want to purchase.

Investment Instrument or Fund Name: Clearly specify the name of the money market instrument or money market fund you intend to invest in. This ensures that your investment is allocated to the correct financial instrument.

Placing the Order: Submit your investment order through your investment account. This can usually be done online or by contacting your broker or financial advisor. The order will be processed, and your funds will be used to purchase the selected money market instrument or allocated to the money market fund.

DIVERSIFICATION FOR RISK MANAGEMENT

As with any investment, diversification is a critical strategy to manage risk. Consider spreading your investments across various money market instruments and issuers to reduce exposure to any single investment. Diversification can enhance the stability of your portfolio and protect your funds from specific risks associated with individual instruments.

By following these steps and maintaining a thoughtful approach to money market investing, you can build a strong foundation for your financial future.

19: MONITORING AND MANAGING MONEY MARKET INVESTMENTS

Monitoring and managing your money market investments are essential to ensure that your portfolio stays aligned with your financial goals and risk tolerance. In this chapter, we'll explore the key aspects of effectively monitoring and managing your money market investments to optimize your returns and maintain financial stability.

STAYING INFORMED WITH MARKET UPDATES

Stay proactive by keeping yourself well-informed about the latest market updates and economic trends. Monitor financial news, interest rate movements, and any changes in economic indicators that may impact money market instruments. Being aware of current market conditions empowers you to make timely decisions and respond to potential opportunities or risks.

REBALANCING YOUR PORTFOLIO

Periodically review your money market investment portfolio to assess its performance and ensure that it remains diversified. Rebalancing involves adjusting the allocation of your investments to maintain your desired risk level and financial goals. If certain money market instruments have outperformed others or if market conditions have changed, rebalancing helps realign your portfolio accordingly.

For money market instruments with credit risk, regularly check the credit ratings of the issuers. Credit rating agencies assess the creditworthiness of issuers, and changes in ratings can signal potential risks or opportunities.

UNDERSTANDING MARKET CONDITIONS AND THEIR IMPACT

Different market conditions can influence money market instruments differently. For example, changes in interest rates can affect the yields of money market funds and fixed-rate instruments like Treasury bills. Understanding how market conditions impact your investments allows you to make strategic decisions and adjust your portfolio when needed.

MATURITY DATES AND REINVESTMENT

For short-term money market instruments like Treasury bills and certificates of deposit, be aware of their maturity dates. As these investments mature, you will have the opportunity to reinvest the proceeds or use them for other financial needs. Evaluating the prevailing market conditions and interest rates will guide you in making informed reinvestment decisions.

MONITORING INTEREST RATE ENVIRONMENT

Interest rates play a significant role in the performance of money market investments. When interest rates rise, yields on money market instruments may become more attractive, potentially impacting your investment decisions. Stay vigilant about interest rate movements and assess how they align with your investment strategy.

ADJUSTING TO CHANGING GOALS AND RISK TOLERANCE

As your financial goals and risk tolerance may change over time, reassess your money market investment strategy accordingly. A change in your life circumstances, investment horizon, or financial objectives might prompt adjustments to your money market holdings.

SEEKING PROFESSIONAL GUIDANCE

Consider seeking guidance from financial advisors or money market experts. Financial professionals can provide valuable insights, assist you in making informed decisions, and help you navigate complex market scenarios.

By actively monitoring and managing your money market investments, you can optimize your portfolio's performance while staying in control of your financial future. Keep yourself informed, review your investment strategy regularly, and be prepared to make adjustments based on market conditions and your evolving financial goals. Staying engaged with your investments is key to building a resilient and rewarding money market investment experience.

20: TAX CONSIDERATIONS FOR MONEY MARKET INVESTMENTS

As a prudent investor, it's essential to understand the tax implications of your money market investments. This chapter explores the key tax considerations related to money market investments, helping you make informed decisions that align with your financial goals while minimizing tax liabilities.

TAXATION OF MONEY MARKET GAINS

When it comes to money market investments, the tax treatment of gains varies depending on the type of instrument and your country's tax laws. Here are some general guidelines to consider:

Interest Income: Interest earned from money market instruments, such as Treasury bills and Certificates of Deposit, is generally considered taxable income. It is usually taxed at your regular income tax rate.

Capital Gains: If you hold money market instruments that are subject to capital gains tax, any profit made from selling these investments at a higher price than the purchase price will be subject to capital gains tax. However, many money market instruments have fixed maturities, so they are not typically subject to capital gains tax.

Capital Losses: If you sell money market instruments at a loss, you may be able to use those capital losses to offset capital gains in the same tax year. If your capital losses exceed your capital gains, you may be able to use the excess losses to offset other taxable income, up to certain limits.

Tax Reporting: Financial institutions and brokerage firms issue tax statements that summarize the interest income earned from money market investments during the tax year. These statements are crucial for accurately reporting your income and complying with tax regulations.

TAX-EXEMPT AND TAX-ADVANTAGED MONEY MARKET OPTIONS

In some countries, certain money market instruments may offer tax advantages or exemptions to investors. Here are some common tax-advantaged or tax-exempt money market options:

Tax-Exempt Money Market Funds: These funds invest in municipal securities issued by state and local governments. The interest income generated from these funds is usually exempt from federal income tax and, in some cases, may also be exempt from state and local taxes.

Tax-Advantaged Retirement Accounts: In some countries, investments in money market instruments within tax-advantaged retirement accounts, such as Individual Retirement Accounts (IRAs) or 401(k) plans, may offer tax benefits. Interest income and capital gains within these accounts can grow tax-deferred or may even be tax-free in retirement.

Education Savings Accounts: Similarly, contributions to education savings accounts, like 529 plans or Education Savings Accounts (ESAs), may offer tax advantages when used for qualified educational expenses. Money market investments within these accounts may grow tax-free, providing potential tax savings for educational purposes.

CONSIDERATION OF MARGINAL TAX RATE

When evaluating the tax implications of money market investments, consider your marginal tax rate—the tax rate applied to the last dollar of your income. Understanding your marginal tax rate will help you assess the true impact of taxes on your money market gains and make well-informed decisions.

TAX-EFFICIENT INVESTING STRATEGIES:

To optimize your after-tax returns, consider implementing tax-efficient investing strategies. For example, you might allocate tax-exempt money market funds to taxable accounts and taxable money market investments to tax-advantaged accounts. This approach can help you maximize tax benefits while maintaining a diversified money market portfolio.

SEEKING PROFESSIONAL TAX ADVICE:

Tax laws and regulations can be complex and subject to change. To ensure compliance with tax laws and maximize your tax advantages, consider seeking advice from a qualified tax professional or financial advisor. They can offer personalized guidance based on your specific financial situation and investment objectives.

By understanding the tax considerations for money market investments and leveraging tax-efficient strategies, you can make smart investment decisions that not only preserve your capital but also optimize your after-tax returns. Stay informed about tax laws and seek professional advice to ensure you stay on track with your financial goals.

21: TIPS FOR SUCCESS IN MONEY MARKET INVESTING

In this chapter, we will share valuable tips to help you succeed in money market investing. Whether you are a new investor or have some experience, these best practices and insights will guide you toward making informed decisions and achieving your financial goals.

BEST PRACTICES FOR NEW INVESTORS

Educate Yourself: Take the time to learn about the different money market instruments and how they work. Understand the risks and rewards associated with each type of investment. Knowledge is your most powerful asset when it comes to successful investing.

Start with Low-Risk Instruments: For beginners, it's prudent to begin with low-risk money market instruments like Treasury bills and money market funds. These options provide stability and safety while you gain confidence and experience in the market.

Define Your Financial Goals: Determine your investment objectives and time horizon. Are you saving for a short-term goal or building wealth for the long term? Knowing your financial goals will help shape your investment strategy.

Establish an Emergency Fund: Before diving into money market investments, ensure you have an emergency fund with enough cash to cover unexpected expenses. This safety net will protect you from needing to liquidate investments during market downturns.

Diversify Your Portfolio: Diversification is a fundamental principle of investing. Spread your money across different money market instruments and issuers to mitigate risks and enhance the stability of your portfolio.

Stay Disciplined: Avoid making impulsive decisions based on short-term market fluctuations. Stick to your investment plan and remain focused on your long-term goals.

LEARNING FROM MISTAKES AND IMPROVING YOUR STRATEGY:

Review Past Decisions: Take the time to assess your investment decisions and their outcomes. Analyze both successful and unsuccessful investments to identify patterns and learn from your experiences.

Adapt to Changing Market Conditions: Financial markets are dynamic and subject to change. Be flexible in your investment approach and adapt your strategy to current market conditions and economic trends.

Seek Guidance from Experts: Don't hesitate to seek advice from financial professionals or seasoned investors. Learning from experienced individuals can provide valuable insights and help you make wiser choices.

Monitor and Adjust: Regularly monitor the performance of your money market investments and review your investment strategy. As your financial goals or risk tolerance change, be prepared to adjust your portfolio accordingly.

Avoid Emotional Investing: Emotional decisions often lead to poor investment choices. Keep your emotions in check and rely on data, research, and logical analysis when making investment decisions.

Continuously Educate Yourself: Money market investing is an ongoing learning process. Stay updated on financial news, economic trends, and changes in the money market landscape to enhance your investment knowledge.

Successful money market investing requires patience, discipline, and a long-term perspective. As you gain experience and learn from your journey, you will become a more confident and astute investor. Embrace the learning process, remain proactive, and let your financial goals guide you toward a prosperous money market investment experience.

22: BEYOND MONEY MARKET
EXPLORING OTHER INVESTMENT OPPORTUNITIES

B y now, you have a solid grasp of money market investing. While money market investments offer safety and liquidity, expanding your investment horizon to explore other opportunities can diversify your portfolio and potentially enhance your returns. In this chapter, we'll explore various investment options beyond money market instruments to consider as part of your overall investment strategy.

LONG-TERM INVESTMENT OPTIONS

Stocks: Investing in stocks represents ownership in a company. Stocks have the potential for significant long-term growth but also come with higher risk compared to money market instruments. They can provide capital appreciation and may pay dividends to shareholders.

Bonds and Fixed-Income Securities: Bonds are debt securities issued by governments, municipalities, or corporations. They offer regular interest payments and return the principal amount at maturity. Bonds are generally considered less risky than stocks but may have longer investment horizons. Treasury bonds, corporate bonds, municipal bonds, and government agency bonds are examples of fixed-income securities.

Certificates of Deposit (CDs) with Longer Maturities: While traditional CDs are short-term money market instruments, longer-term CDs with higher interest rates can offer a safe and fixed return for longer investment horizons.

Mutual Funds and Exchange-Traded Funds (ETFs): Mutual funds and ETFs pool funds from multiple investors to invest in a diversified portfolio of securities, such as stocks, bonds, or a combination of both. These funds offer convenience, professional management, and diversification, making them suitable for those seeking broader exposure to different asset classes.

Real Estate Investments: Real estate investments involve buying properties or investing in Real Estate Investment Trusts (REITs) that own and manage real estate properties. Real estate investments can provide rental income and the potential for property appreciation.

Index Funds and Passive Investing: Index funds are a type of mutual fund or ETF that aims to replicate the performance of a specific market index, such as the S&P 500. Passive investing in index funds offers low fees and broad market exposure.

Exchange-Traded Notes (ETNs) and Commodities: ETNs are debt securities that offer exposure to the performance of an underlying index or asset, such as commodities. Commodities, such as gold, oil, or agricultural products, can serve as a hedge against inflation and provide diversification.

Retirement Accounts (IRA, 401(k), etc.): Take advantage of tax-advantaged retirement accounts, such as Individual Retirement Accounts (IRA) and employer-sponsored 401(k) plans. These accounts offer tax benefits and allow for a wide range of investment choices.

Peer-to-Peer Lending and Alternative Investments: Explore alternative investments like peer-to-peer lending platforms or private equity opportunities. These investments may have higher risk but can potentially offer attractive returns.

Global Investments: Consider diversifying your portfolio with international investments, such as international stocks or global mutual funds, to take advantage of opportunities in different markets.

THE ROLE OF MONEY MARKET IN YOUR OVERALL INVESTMENT PLAN

When you embark on your investment journey, the money market serves as a solid starting point, especially if you are new to investing or prefer a lower-risk approach. Think of the money market as a launching pad, propelling you forward as you gain knowledge and experience, ultimately building the confidence to explore higher-risk opportunities for potentially greater rewards without compromising the stability of your financial security portfolio.

Remember, as you progress in your investment journey, consider allocating more funds toward higher-risk ventures, but only with money that you can afford to lose. Your essential financial obligations like rent, bills, tuition, and emergency funds should remain secure in your financial security portfolio.

Resist the temptation to liquidate your financial security holdings to pursue higher returns. Instead, determine a strategic asset allocation plan that balances your investments between the stability of money market instruments and the growth potential of riskier assets. Stay committed to this plan, and as you continue to grow your money, diversify across your security and growth portfolios.

By starting with the money market and gradually expanding your investment horizons, you can steadily build a strong and resilient investment portfolio. Always keep in mind your financial goals, risk tolerance, and long-term objectives, seeking opportunities for growth while safeguarding your financial security. With discipline and patience, your investment journey will lead to financial success and empowerment.

Building a well-rounded investment portfolio involves understanding your financial goals, risk tolerance, and investment time horizon. Each investment opportunity serves a specific purpose within your overall plan. As you explore other investment options beyond the money market, consider seeking advice from financial professionals to tailor a strategy that aligns with your unique circumstances and aspirations. A diversified and balanced investment approach will help you navigate the financial landscape with confidence and work towards your long-term financial success.

23: CONTINUED LEARNING AND GROWTH

As an investor, the learning process is never-ending. This chapter emphasizes the importance of continued learning and personal growth, equipping you with the knowledge and tools to evolve as an informed and savvy investor. In the world of finance and investing, knowledge is a powerful tool.

As you embark on your journey to build and manage your investment portfolio, continuous learning and growth are essential for achieving long-term success. This chapter emphasizes the importance of ongoing education and provides guidance on how to expand your financial knowledge and refine your investment strategies.

STAY UPDATED WITH FINANCIAL NEWS

Keep abreast of the latest financial news and market developments. Regularly read reputable financial publications, follow financial websites, and watch market analysis programs. Staying informed about economic trends, policy changes, and global events will help you make well-informed investment decisions.

Follow financial experts, analysts, and reputable sources on social media or financial news platforms. Their insights can offer valuable perspectives on market dynamics and investment strategies.

ATTEND INVESTMENT WORKSHOPS AND SEMINARS

Investment workshops and seminars offer valuable insights from industry experts and seasoned investors. Consider participating in these events to deepen your understanding of various investment strategies, asset classes, and market dynamics.

Enroll in online courses or attend webinars offered by financial institutions, universities, or investment firms. These educational resources can enhance your investment knowledge.

JOIN INVESTMENT FORUMS AND COMMUNITIES

Engage with like-minded investors by joining investment forums and online communities. Participating in discussions and sharing experiences can broaden your perspective and provide fresh insights into investment opportunities.

READ BOOKS ON INVESTING

Expand your knowledge by reading books written by renowned investors and financial experts. Books on investment strategies, economic theories, and success stories can offer valuable lessons and guidance.

ANALYZE INVESTMENT PERFORMANCE

Regularly review the performance of your investments, both in the money market and other asset classes. Analyzing past performance can help you identify patterns, understand what worked well, and learn from any mistakes made.

As your financial goals or life circumstances change, be open to adjusting your investment strategy accordingly. Flexibility is essential for long-term success.

SEEK PROFESSIONAL ADVICE

Consider consulting with a financial advisor or investment professional for personalized guidance. A qualified advisor can help you align your investment strategy with your financial goals and risk tolerance, tailoring a plan that suits your individual needs.

EMBRACE TECHNOLOGY

Explore investment apps and platforms that offer advanced tools for portfolio tracking, analysis, and research. Embracing technology can streamline your investment process and provide real-time data to aid decision-making.

LEARN FROM MISTAKES

Accept that investing involves risk, and mistakes are a natural part of the process. Instead of dwelling on errors, view them as opportunities for growth and learning. Assess what went wrong, adjust your strategy, and move forward with renewed confidence.

Investing requires patience and discipline. Avoid making emotional decisions and stick to your well-thought-out investment plan.

By prioritizing continued learning and growth, you can become a more informed and confident investor. Stay curious, seek knowledge from reputable sources, and remain open to new ideas and perspectives. Investing is a lifelong journey, and with dedication and ongoing education, you can enhance your financial literacy and make well-informed decisions to achieve your financial goals.

CONCLUSION

Congratulations on completing "Money Market Investing 101: A Beginner's Guide to Low-Risk Short-Term Investments." We hope this comprehensive journey has equipped you with valuable knowledge and insights into the world of money market investments and beyond. As you now conclude this book, let's recap the key takeaways and set the stage for your continued success as an investor.

Throughout this guide, you've gained a solid understanding of the money market, a vital component of the financial landscape known for its low-risk, short-term investment opportunities. We explored various money market instruments, such as Treasury Bills, Certificates of Deposit (CDs), Commercial Paper, Repurchase Agreements (Repos), Money Market Funds, Municipal Notes, Banker's Acceptances (BAs), Eurodollars, Floating Rate Notes (FRNs), Treasury Money Market Mutual Funds (TMMFs), Tax-Exempt Commercial Paper, and Asset-Backed Commercial Paper (ABCP).

Each instrument offers distinct features and benefits, enabling you to tailor your investments to match your financial objectives and risk tolerance.

Additionally, we dived into essential aspects of money market investing, such as assessing risk, building investment strategies, understanding tax considerations, and managing your money market portfolio effectively. Armed with this knowledge, you have the tools to make informed decisions, protect your capital, and strive for steady returns.

Moreover, this book has taken you beyond the money market to explore various long-term investment options, such as stocks, bonds, real estate, mutual funds, and ETFs. Understanding these broader investment opportunities allows you to diversify your portfolio, maximize potential returns, and achieve your financial goals.

Remember, investing is a journey that requires ongoing learning and growth. Stay informed, embrace new opportunities, and remain disciplined in your approach. Whether you are a novice investor or a seasoned pro, continuous education and adaptation are key to thriving in the dynamic financial markets.

As you move forward, I encourage you to define your investment goals clearly and align your decisions with those objectives. Seek professional guidance when needed, but also trust your knowledge and intuition to make sound investment choices.

Lastly, always prioritize your financial security by maintaining an emergency fund and investing money you can afford to put at risk. Let your money market investments serve as a foundation for your financial success, providing stability and liquidity as you explore additional opportunities for growth.

Thank you for choosing "Money Market Investing 101: A Beginner's Guide to Low-Risk Short-Term Investments." May your investment journey be filled with prosperity, wisdom, and fulfillment.

As you continue to grow your wealth, remember that financial success is a product of dedication, patience, and informed decision-making. Happy investing, and may your future be filled with endless possibilities.

ABOUT THE AUTHOR

Usiere Uko

Usiere Uko is a Consultant, ILO Certified Trainer, and Business & Finance Author focused on financial independence and entrepreneurship. A former oil and gas engineer turned entrepreneur, he helps individuals and business owners build sustainable income, make smarter financial decisions, and grow resilient businesses.

He is a certified Business Development Service Provider (BDSP) and an ILO-certified trainer in SIYB and WIDB, and currently serves as Lead Consultant at Sageway Consulting and Training Coordinator at The Citadel Business Academy.

Usiere writes in a friendly and practical style, making complex financial and business ideas simple, clear, and actionable for everyday readers and entrepreneurs. He is based in Lagos, Nigeria.

BOOKS IN THIS SERIES

SAFE INCOME INVESTING MASTERY

Money Market Investing 101: A Beginner's Guide To Low-Risk Short-Term Investments

Treasury Bill Investing 101: Your Essential Step-By-Step Guide To Building Financial Security

Treasury Bonds Investing 101: A Beginner's Guide To Low-Risk Investment Strategies

Treasury Notes Investing 101: Step-By-Step Guide And Smart Investor Starter's Handbook

Treasury Tips Investing 101: Protect Your Money From Inflation With Government-Backed Securities

BOOKS BY THIS AUTHOR

Practical Steps To Financial Freedom And Independence: Money Management Skills For Beginners

Before You Trade Forex: Things You Need To Know If You Desire To Start Trading Forex Profitably

Before You Invest In Cryptocurrency: A Simple Guide To Understanding The Cryptocurrency Market

101 Common Money Mistakes To Avoid: And How To Fix Them. Book 1: Expenses. Money Management, Making Your Budget Work

How To Avoid Living Under Financial Pressure: A Simple Guide To Getting Back Control Of Your Finances

Financial Independence For Employees: Making Your Job A Stepping Stone To Exiting The Rat Race

And Living Your Dreams

Managing Your Money Post Covid: Financial
Management Skills For An Era Of High Inflation
And Market Disruption

Retire On Your Own Terms: A Simple Guide To
Financially Literate Retirement Planning

Your Ultimate Money Makeover: Manage Your
Money Better, Take Control Of Your Finances And
Your Life

Teaching Kids Money 101: Simple Parenting
Strategies For Raising Financially Literate Kids
From Toddler To Teen Years And Beyond

Uncle Ben's Money Lessons: Book I: Do You Want
To Work For Money? A Vacation Story With An
Adventure Into The World Of Money

Nft Investing 101: A Beginner's Guide To
Collectible Digital Assets

Stock Market Investing 101: A Practical Beginners
Guide To Online And Offline Stock Trading

Investing In Etfs 101: A Beginner's Guide For Building Wealth With Exchange-Traded Funds

Day Trading 101: A Complete Beginner's Guide To Trading The Markets

Forex Trading 101: A Beginner's Guide And Strategies To Profitable Currency Trading

Options Trading 101: A Beginner's Guide To Trading Stock Options

Futures Trading 101: A Step-By-Step Guide And Strategies For Beginner Traders